DRAWING LIFE
IN
MOTION

BY JIM ARNOSKY

Lothrop, Lee & Shepard Books   New York

Library of Congress Cataloging in Publication Data. Arnosky, Jim. Drawing life in motion. Summary: Instructions for drawing plants and animals in motion. 1. Action in art. 2. Drawing—Technique. [1. Botanical illustration—Technique. 2. Animal painting and illustration—Technique. 3. Drawing—Technique] I. Title. NC785.A76 1984   743′.6   83-25129   ISBN 0-688-02714-8   ISBN 0-688-07076-0 (pbk.)

To my father,
whose precise, logical, lovely
drawings of machines in motion
were my first lessons
in line art.

Plants and animals are privileged characters. They are the only things that have the power to make themselves move. Every movement they perform is an expression of life.

This little book is an expression of the life I feel in me and see moving all around me.

Jim Arnosky
Ramtails, 1984

Every spring, seeds of a wild vine sprout near our woodshed. It is the beginning of a slow, subtle dance, each day covering more of the shed's weathered wall with its moves. It is an act of creation, performed in the continuous motion of growth—from seed to twining stem, leaf to curling tendril, bloom to fruit, to seed again.

While growing, individual plant parts make incidental movements whenever they are stimulated by gravity, light, or touch. These movements are called tropisms.

PLANT MOVEMENTS STIMULATED BY GRAVITY ARE CALLED GEOTROPISMS (EARTH-BENDING)

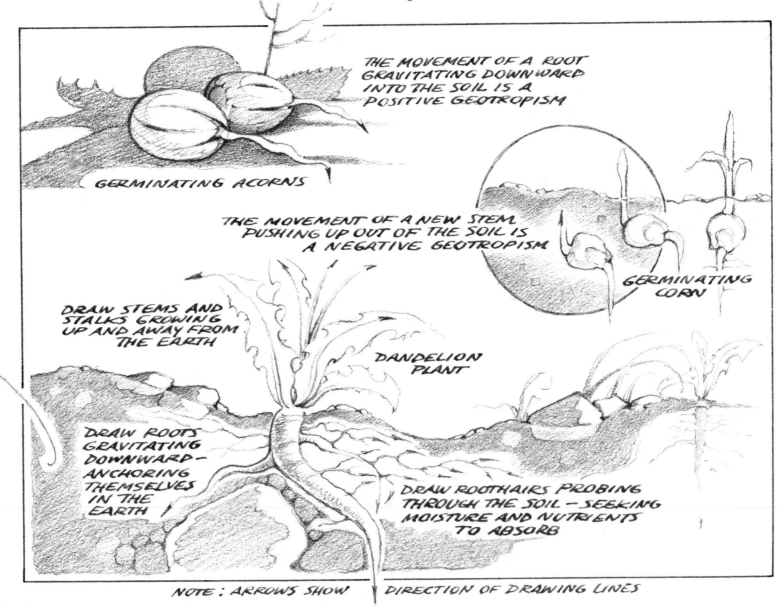

THE MOVEMENT OF A ROOT GRAVITATING DOWNWARD INTO THE SOIL IS A POSITIVE GEOTROPISM

GERMINATING ACORNS

THE MOVEMENT OF A NEW STEM PUSHING UP OUT OF THE SOIL IS A NEGATIVE GEOTROPISM

GERMINATING CORN

DRAW STEMS AND STALKS GROWING UP AND AWAY FROM THE EARTH

DANDELION PLANT

DRAW ROOTS GRAVITATING DOWNWARD — ANCHORING THEMSELVES IN THE EARTH

DRAW ROOTHAIRS PROBING THROUGH THE SOIL — SEEKING MOISTURE AND NUTRIENTS TO ABSORB

NOTE: ARROWS SHOW DIRECTION OF DRAWING LINES

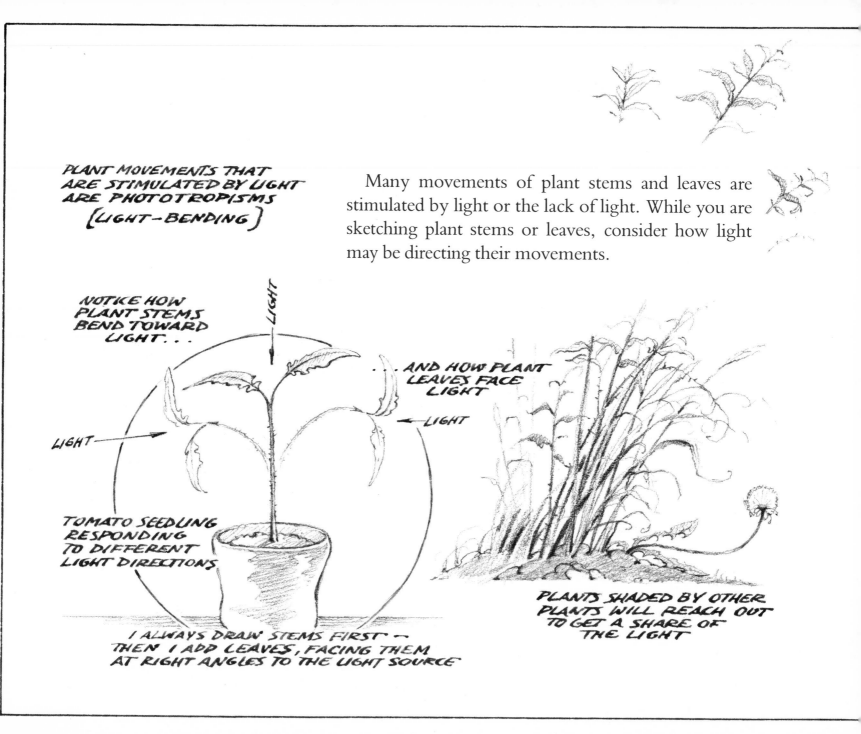

PLANT MOVEMENTS THAT ARE STIMULATED BY LIGHT ARE PHOTOTROPISMS (LIGHT-BENDING)

Many movements of plant stems and leaves are stimulated by light or the lack of light. While you are sketching plant stems or leaves, consider how light may be directing their movements.

NOTICE HOW PLANT STEMS BEND TOWARD LIGHT...

LIGHT

...AND HOW PLANT LEAVES FACE LIGHT

LIGHT

LIGHT

TOMATO SEEDLING RESPONDING TO DIFFERENT LIGHT DIRECTIONS

I ALWAYS DRAW STEMS FIRST — THEN I ADD LEAVES, FACING THEM AT RIGHT ANGLES TO THE LIGHT SOURCE

PLANTS SHADED BY OTHER PLANTS WILL REACH OUT TO GET A SHARE OF THE LIGHT

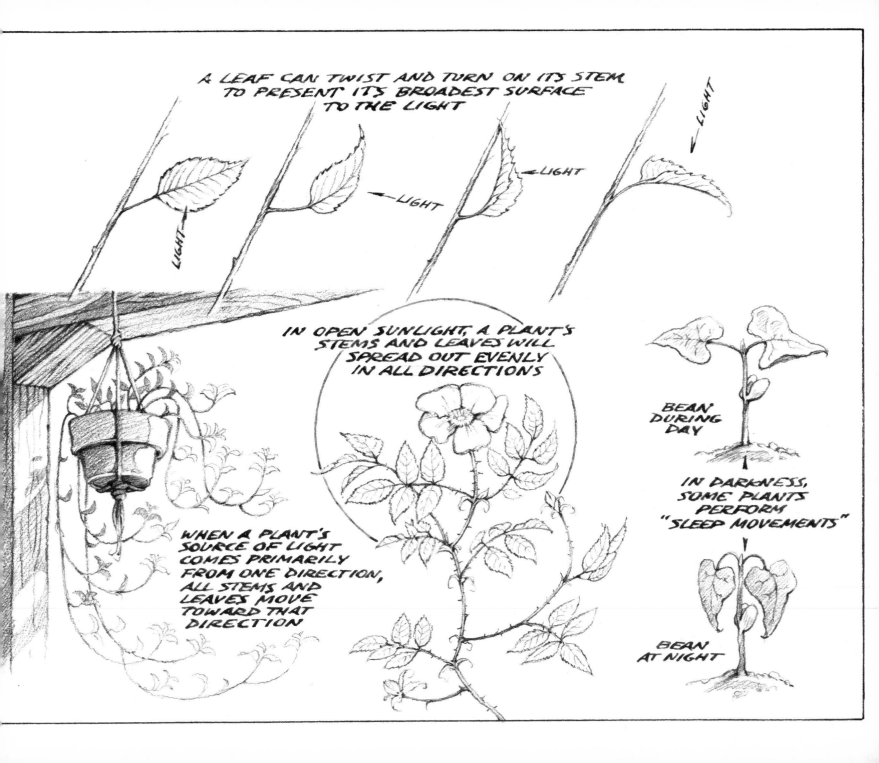

A LEAF CAN TWIST AND TURN ON ITS STEM
TO PRESENT ITS BROADEST SURFACE
TO THE LIGHT

←LIGHT

←LIGHT

←LIGHT

←LIGHT

IN OPEN SUNLIGHT, A PLANT'S
STEMS AND LEAVES WILL
SPREAD OUT EVENLY
IN ALL DIRECTIONS

WHEN A PLANT'S
SOURCE OF LIGHT
COMES PRIMARILY
FROM ONE DIRECTION,
ALL STEMS AND
LEAVES MOVE
TOWARD THAT
DIRECTION

BEAN
DURING
DAY

IN DARKNESS,
SOME PLANTS
PERFORM
"SLEEP MOVEMENTS"

BEAN
AT NIGHT

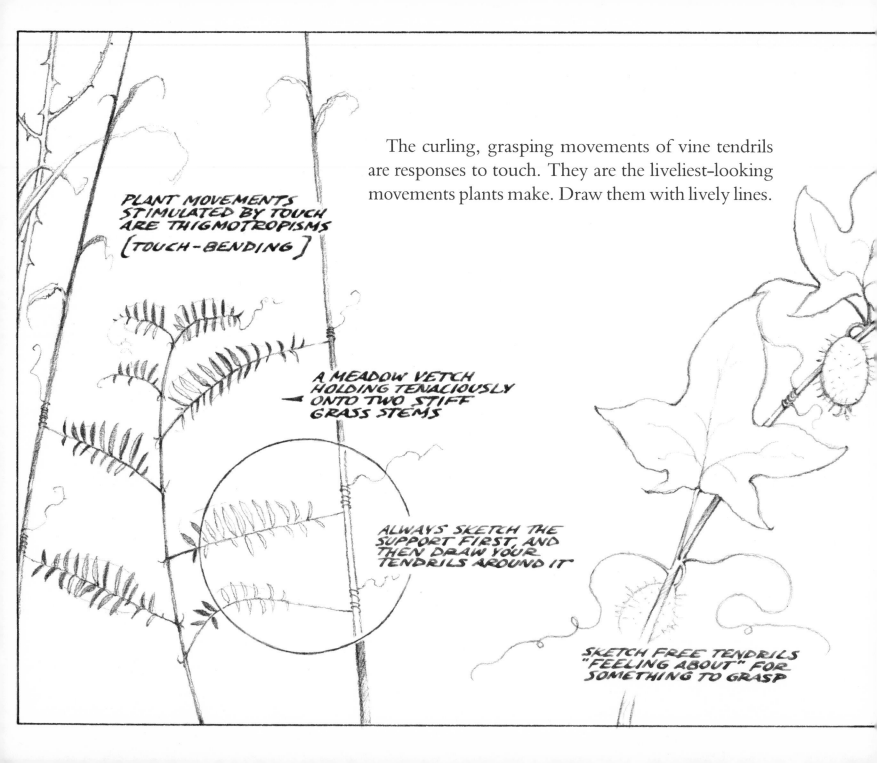

The curling, grasping movements of vine tendrils are responses to touch. They are the liveliest-looking movements plants make. Draw them with lively lines.

PLANT MOVEMENTS STIMULATED BY TOUCH ARE THIGMOTROPISMS [TOUCH-BENDING]

A MEADOW VETCH HOLDING TENACIOUSLY ONTO TWO STIFF GRASS STEMS

ALWAYS SKETCH THE SUPPORT FIRST, AND THEN DRAW YOUR TENDRILS AROUND IT

SKETCH FREE TENDRILS "FEELING ABOUT" FOR SOMETHING TO GRASP

ONCE A TENDRIL HAS A FIRM HOLD ON A SUPPORT. . . .

PULL

. . . IT WILL CURL ITSELF, PULLING THE WHOLE PLANT STEM TOWARD THE SUPPORT

WILD CUCUMBER

THE TWINING CLIMB OF CERTAIN PLANTS IS THE RESULT OF STEMS BENDING TO THE TOUCH OF A SUPPORT WHILE ALSO GROWING HIGHER AND HIGHER

POLE BEAN

PULL

THE MORE CURLS YOU DRAW, THE MORE PULL YOU SUGGEST

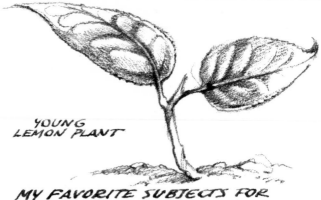

YOUNG
LEMON PLANT

MY FAVORITE SUBJECTS FOR
THIS KIND OF SKETCHING
EXPERIMENT ARE VERY
YOUNG PLANTS BECAUSE
THEY ARE SMALL ENOUGH
FOR ME TO WATCH ALL OF
THEIR PARTS CLOSELY FOR
ANY SIGN OF MOVEMENT.

Choose an individual plant around your house and sketch it from the same view once every hour or so for one whole afternoon. At the end of the day, compare your sketches to see how the plant has moved. Some of the plants you choose to sketch may move very little. Some may move a lot.

My favorite subjects for this kind of sketching experiment are very young plants because they are small enough for me to watch all of their parts closely for any sign of movement.

LEAF BUDS ERUPTING
IN GROWTH

IN OLDER PLANTS, I WATCH
PARTS THAT ARE IN AN
IMPORTANT STAGE OF
DEVELOPMENT, SUCH AS
BUDS ERUPTING AND
NEW LEAVES UNFOLDING

NEW LEAVES UNFOLDING
FROM THE CENTER
OF A STRAWBERRY
PLANT

PERIODIC SKETCHES OF
A PICKLE PLANT

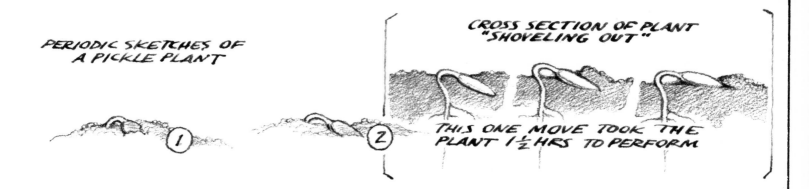

CROSS SECTION OF PLANT
"SHOVELING OUT"

THIS ONE MOVE TOOK THE
PLANT 1½ HRS TO PERFORM

I spent one sunny day in the garden making periodic sketches of a pickle plant.

My first sketch showed the tiny sprout just beginning to appear above the ground. My second sketch pictured it shoveling up through the sandy soil.

Subsequent sketches showed the slow motion of the plant pulling its seedling leaves out of their seed case.

My last sketch was of the little pickle plant holding its closed seedling leaves up off the garden floor.

SEED CASE

SEEDLING LEAVES PULLING
OUT OF SEED CASE

LEAVES JUST BEGINNING
TO SPREAD OPEN

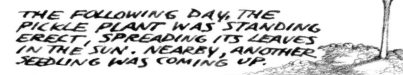

THE FOLLOWING DAY, THE
PICKLE PLANT WAS STANDING
ERECT, SPREADING ITS LEAVES
IN THE SUN. NEARBY, ANOTHER
SEEDLING WAS COMING UP.

Animals move freely. Many are conscious of where and why they move. Life is moving around them. They can sense it. Life is pulsing within them. They can hardly contain it. Even when standing still, animals move with breaths or blinks, always ready for action.

You can breathe life into your drawings of still animals by giving them a look of awareness or by poising some part of their bodies on the verge of, or at the end of, a move.

IN YOUR DRAWINGS OF ANIMALS, MAKE IT CLEAR THAT THEY ARE AWARE OF THE WORLD AROUND THEM...

...THROUGH THEIR SENSES OF SIGHT,

HEARING,

SMELL,

OR TOUCH.

WHILE A CAT IS
DOZING, AN ARCH
IN ITS BACK OR
CURL IN ITS TAIL
SUGGESTS ENERGY
REPOSING

A tilted head, expressive face, arched back, or curved tail can make an animal look as though it might break the spell of stillness at any moment, by blinking an eye, heaving a breath, or moving away.

AN OPENED BEAK, LIFTED
WING OR RAISED CREST
CAN PERK UP A DRAWING
OF A PERCHED BIRD

Animals can move from place to place by pushing or pulling on other things. An inchworm crawls by pushing against the ground with its hind end and then pulling on the ground with its front end.

A toad's muscular hind legs push against the ground with every hop. A lizard climbing up a boulder pulls on the rock with each clawed step.

The most effective way I know to draw animals in motion is to show them in the midst of pushing or pulling themselves along.

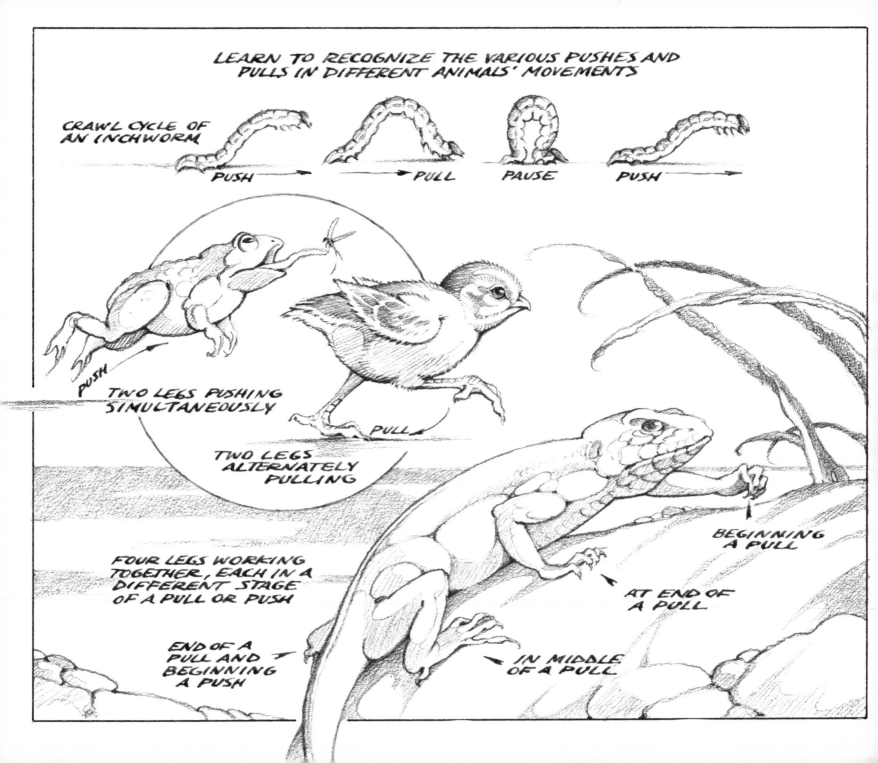

LEARN TO RECOGNIZE THE VARIOUS PUSHES AND
PULLS IN DIFFERENT ANIMALS' MOVEMENTS

CRAWL CYCLE OF
AN INCHWORM

PUSH → → PULL PAUSE PUSH →

PUSH

TWO LEGS PUSHING
SIMULTANEOUSLY

PULL

TWO LEGS
ALTERNATELY
PULLING

FOUR LEGS WORKING
TOGETHER, EACH IN A
DIFFERENT STAGE
OF A PULL OR PUSH

BEGINNING
A PULL

AT END OF
A PULL

END OF A
PULL AND
BEGINNING
A PUSH

IN MIDDLE
OF A PULL

EVERY ANIMAL PERFORMS A VARIETY
OF PUSH AND PULL MOVEMENTS
AS IT GOES ABOUT ITS
DAILY BUSINESS
CONSIDER WHAT THE ANIMALS IN YOUR PICTURES MUST
PUSH OR PULL TO MAKE THE MOVEMENTS YOU ARE DRAWING

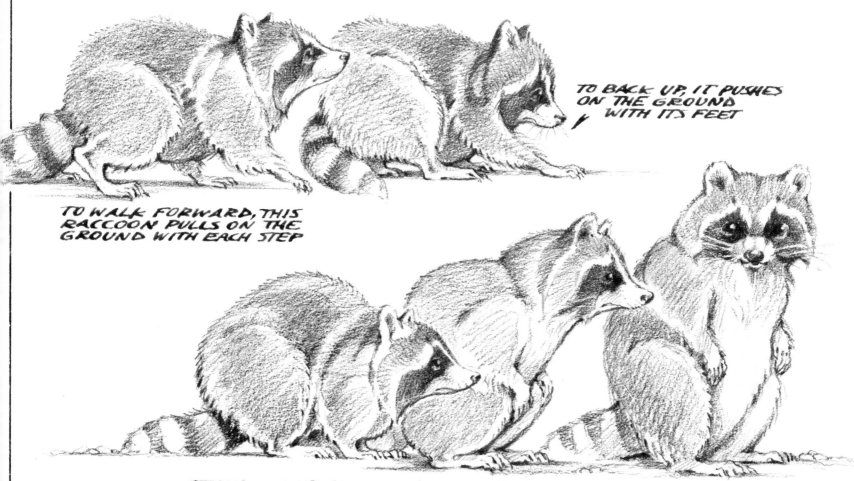

TO BACK UP, IT PUSHES
ON THE GROUND
WITH ITS FEET

TO WALK FORWARD, THIS
RACCOON PULLS ON THE
GROUND WITH EACH STEP

STANDING UP IS A PUSHING MOVEMENT—
FEET AND LEGS PUSHING AGAINST EARTH

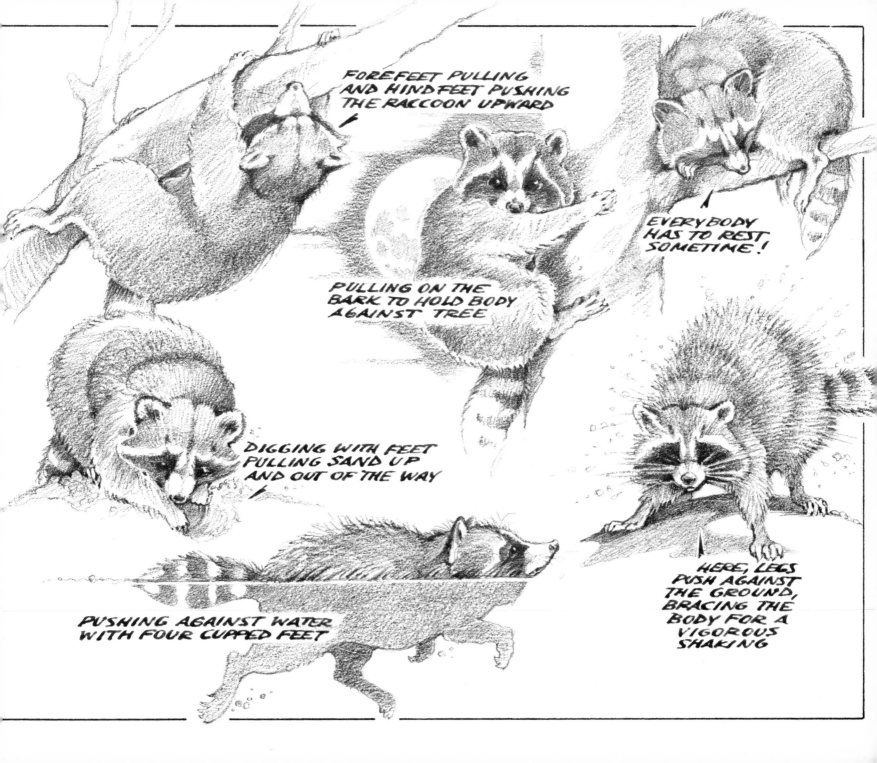

Any movement changes the shape of the shadow being cast. Watch how your own shadow alters as you perform different movements.

MAKE THE SHADOWS IN YOUR DRAWINGS LOOK COMPATIBLE IN SIZE AND SHAPE WITH THE MOVEMENTS OF THE THINGS CASTING THEM

BE SURE THE SHADOWS YOU DRAW FOLLOW THE CONTOURS OF THE SURFACES THEY ARE BEING CAST UPON

DURING A MOVEMENT, WHEREVER PART OF AN ANIMAL'S BODY TOUCHES THE GROUND IT ALSO TOUCHES ITS OWN SHADOW

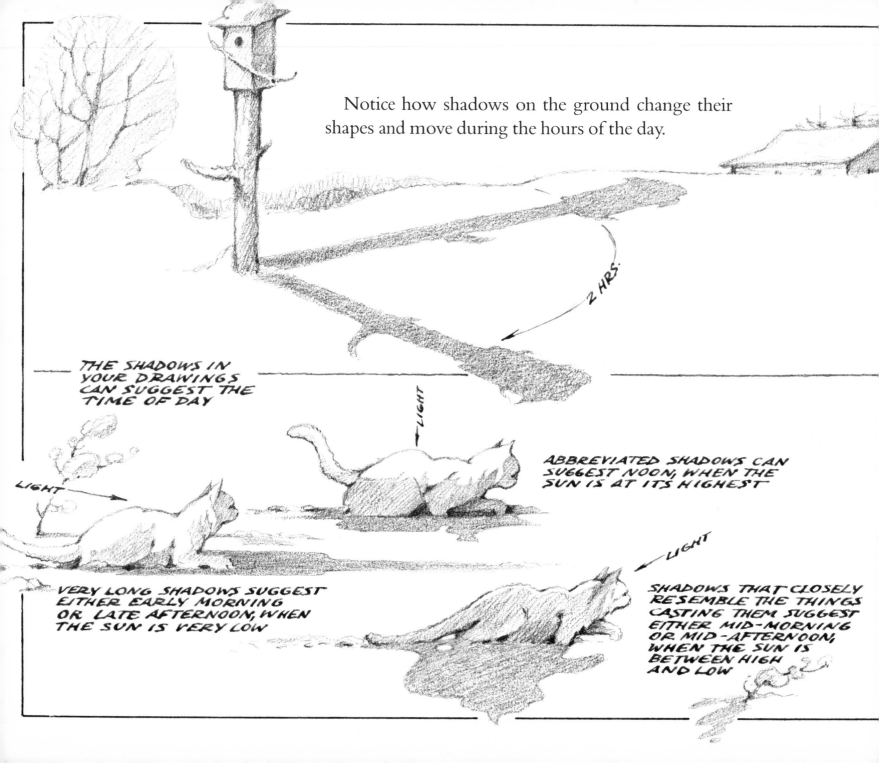

Notice how shadows on the ground change their shapes and move during the hours of the day.

2 HRS.

THE SHADOWS IN YOUR DRAWINGS CAN SUGGEST THE TIME OF DAY

LIGHT

ABBREVIATED SHADOWS CAN SUGGEST NOON, WHEN THE SUN IS AT IT'S HIGHEST

LIGHT

VERY LONG SHADOWS SUGGEST EITHER EARLY MORNING OR LATE AFTERNOON, WHEN THE SUN IS VERY LOW

LIGHT

SHADOWS THAT CLOSELY RESEMBLE THE THINGS CASTING THEM SUGGEST EITHER MID-MORNING OR MID-AFTERNOON, WHEN THE SUN IS BETWEEN HIGH AND LOW

OF COURSE, WHENEVER ANYTHING'S GROUND SHADOW CHANGES, ITS BODY SHADING ALSO CHANGES.

← OUR BEEHIVE IN DECEMBER AT 11:03 A.M. SHOWING HIVE'S BODY SHADING AND SHADOW CAST ON THE GROUND

BEEHIVE AT 1:30 P.M.

Careful attention to shadows underscores the motion of your subjects and simultaneously suggests the motion of the Sun and the Earth.

AT 3:00 P.M.

I love the shadowy look of trout in their streams and the sunny sight when one leaps into air to catch a flying insect.

A trout leaping after an airborne fly is a split-second drama. Capturing such fleeting moments in your outdoor sketches is a challenge. Accurately recording what you see so you can share the experience with others is a joy.

When you are drawing moving animals from life, you must draw quickly to keep up with their action.

Whenever I sketch live, moving animals, I make my drawing lines "reenact" the scene I am seeing.

For example, when I see a trout jumping after a mayfly, I quickly sketch in the water line and the fly. Then I draw the trout in motion as I recall it, "leaping" each line of its body up toward the mayfly.

ONCE YOU'VE GOTTEN THIS FAR, YOU CAN SLOW DOWN AND ADD SOME DETAILS AND SHADING

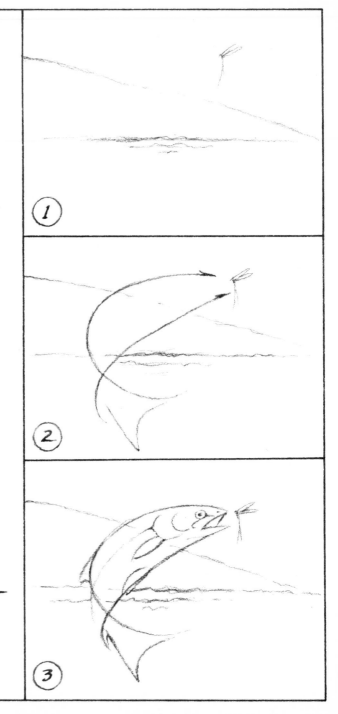

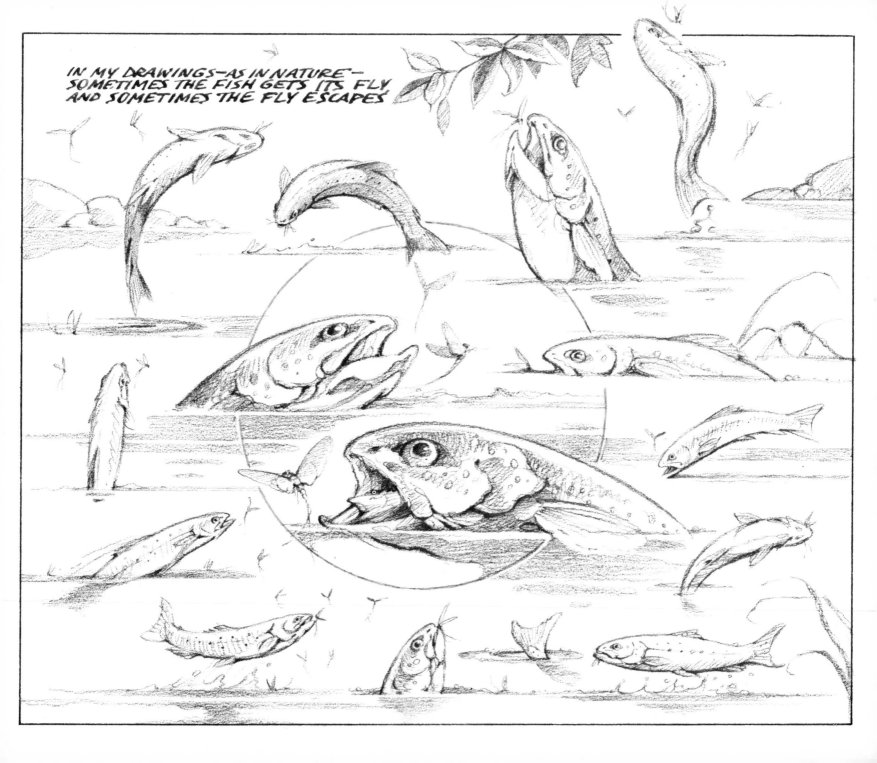

A fish moves underwater in a nearly weightless state. The density of the water helps hold its body up.

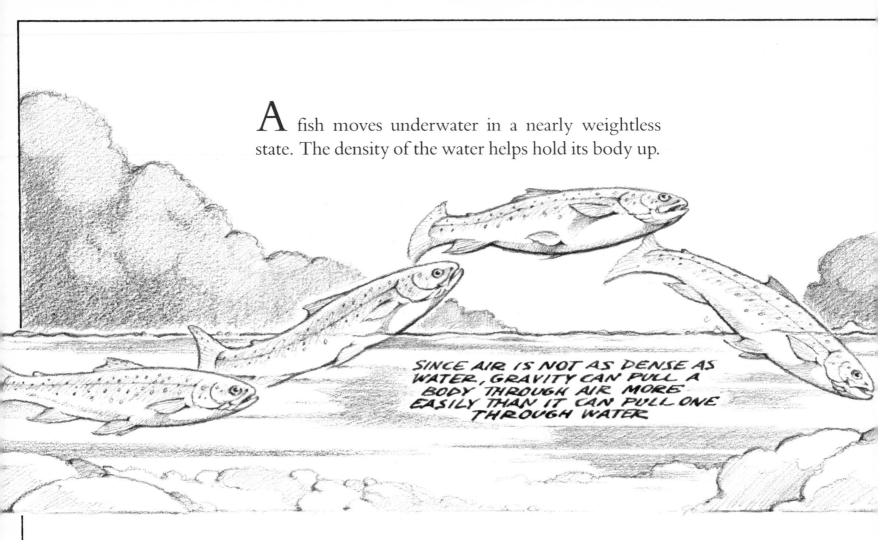

SINCE AIR IS NOT AS DENSE AS WATER, GRAVITY CAN PULL A BODY THROUGH AIR MORE EASILY THAN IT CAN PULL ONE THROUGH WATER

A fish can leap out of water into air but cannot travel through air long before its own body weight pulls it down.

I USE MY HEAVIEST LINES TO SUGGEST ANY BODY WEIGHT BEING SHIFTED, LIFTED, CARRIED OR THROWN.

EWE SHIFTING HER WEIGHT TO PUSH ANOTHER AWAY

SHIFTING WEIGHT TO SCRATCH SIDE ON POST

EWE LIFTING HER WEIGHT TO STAND

HEAVY BODY WEIGHT BEING CARRIED

THESE TWO BUTTING RAMS ARE THROWING THEIR WEIGHT AT EACH OTHER (OUCH!)

SOME THINGS HAVE VERY LITTLE BODY WEIGHT. THEIR MOVEMENTS ARE LIGHT AND AIRY. I USE MY LIGHTEST LINES TO DRAW THEM.

OUTLINE
OF LEAF
[ACTUAL
SIZE]

FALL —

A LEAF'S SIZE AND
SHAPE GREATLY
AFFECT THE WAY
IT WILL FALL

In autumn, find a comfortable spot to sit under some trees and watch their falling leaves. Concentrate on a single leaf at a time and try to recreate its downward dance on paper with your pencil line. You will find that, no matter how the leaf moves or changes course, its fall can be visualized and drawn in one essential line of motion.

As you relax in the rhythm of the falling leaves, your drawing lines will become fresh and light. And you won't run out of subjects until all the trees are bare.

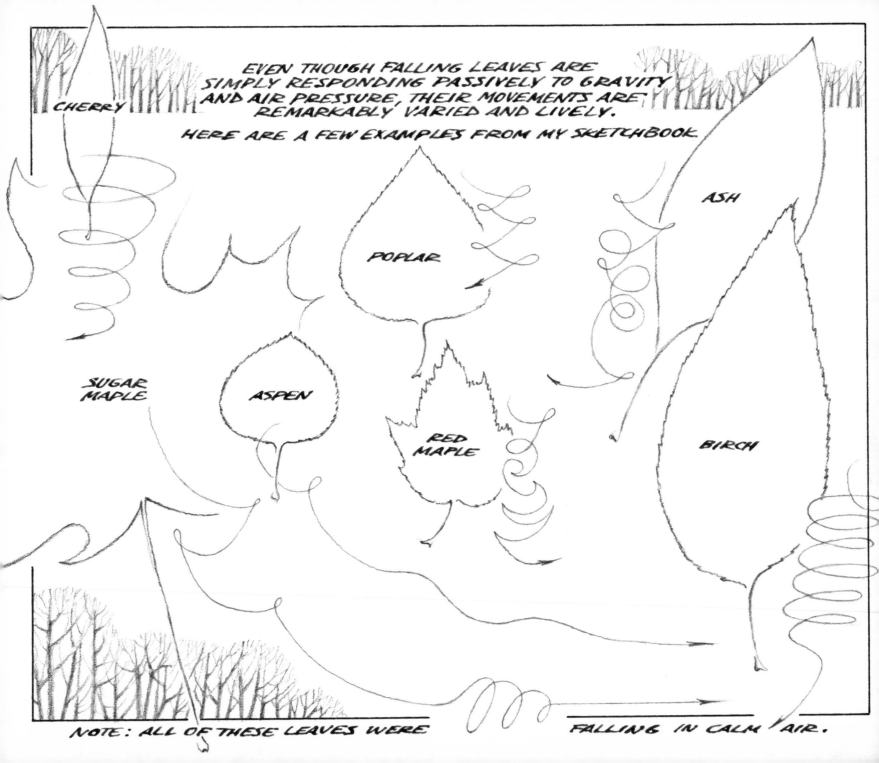

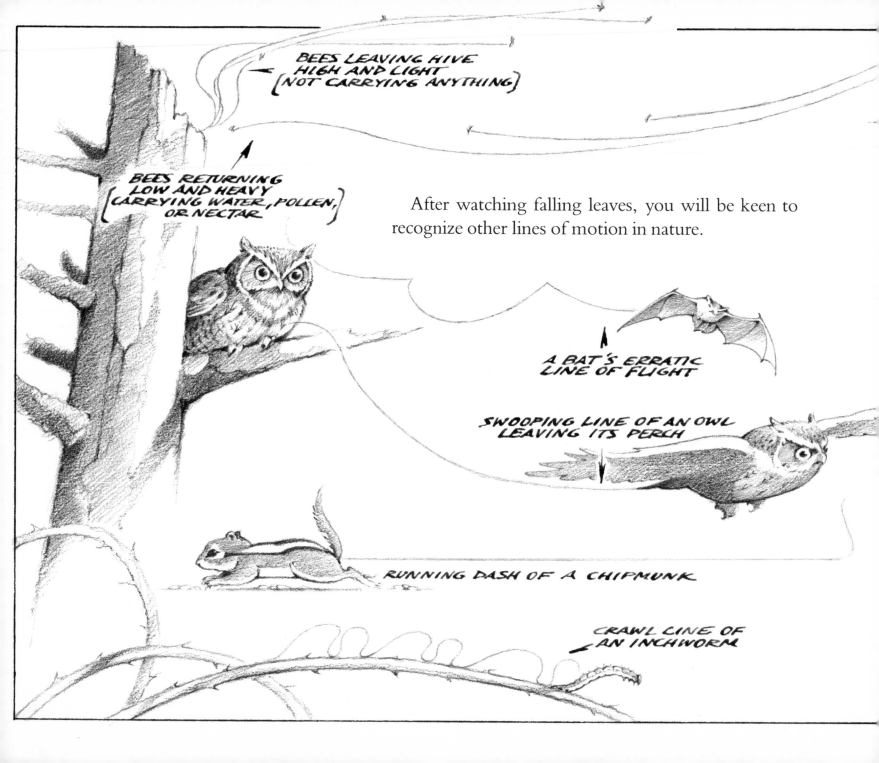

BEES LEAVING HIVE
HIGH AND LIGHT
[NOT CARRYING ANYTHING]

BEES RETURNING
LOW AND HEAVY
[CARRYING WATER, POLLEN,
OR NECTAR]

After watching falling leaves, you will be keen to recognize other lines of motion in nature.

A BAT'S ERRATIC
LINE OF FLIGHT

SWOOPING LINE OF AN OWL
LEAVING ITS PERCH

RUNNING DASH OF A CHIPMUNK

CRAWL LINE OF
AN INCHWORM

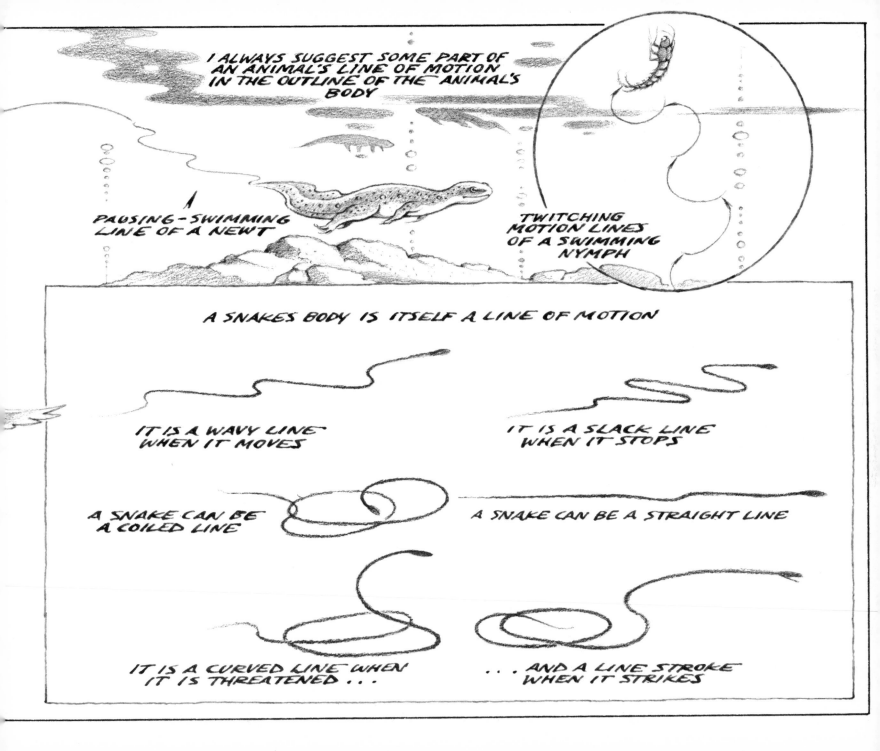

Every line of motion is composed of successive, and often very different, movements. Among them, there is usually one particular movement that best suggests the whole line of motion. That is the movement to look for and to draw!

THIS MOVEMENT, IF DRAWN ALONE, WOULD NOT SUGGEST THE SWIMMING OTTER'S UNDULATING LINE OF MOTION

LIKEWISE, THIS WOULD ONLY LOOK LIKE A DOWNWARD DIVE

All by itself, it will evoke the harmonious sequence of moves that came before and that will follow. A picture of that one movement will become animated by the imagination of anyone who looks at it.

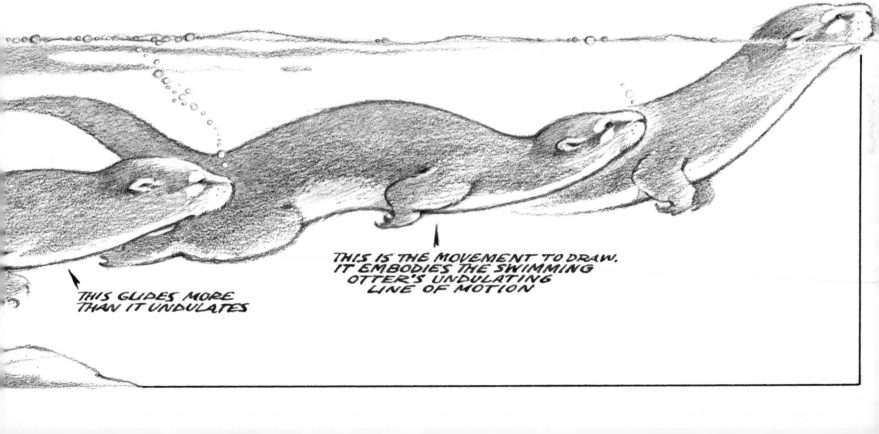

THIS IS THE MOVEMENT TO DRAW.
IT EMBODIES THE SWIMMING
OTTER'S UNDULATING
LINE OF MOTION

THIS GLIDES MORE
THAN IT UNDULATES

ANY MOVEMENT YOU CAN SEE CAN ALSO BE VISUALIZED AS A LINE OF MOTION, REALIZED AS A SEQUENCE OF RELATED MOVES, AND CHARACTERIZED IN ONE PERFECT POSE.

Watch a dog running. As it accelerates, it gains momentum. Its line of motion becomes more direct.

When you draw an animal moving fast, you have to show that only friction slowing it up, gravity pulling it down, something solid blocking its way, or its own muscular effort can stop it.

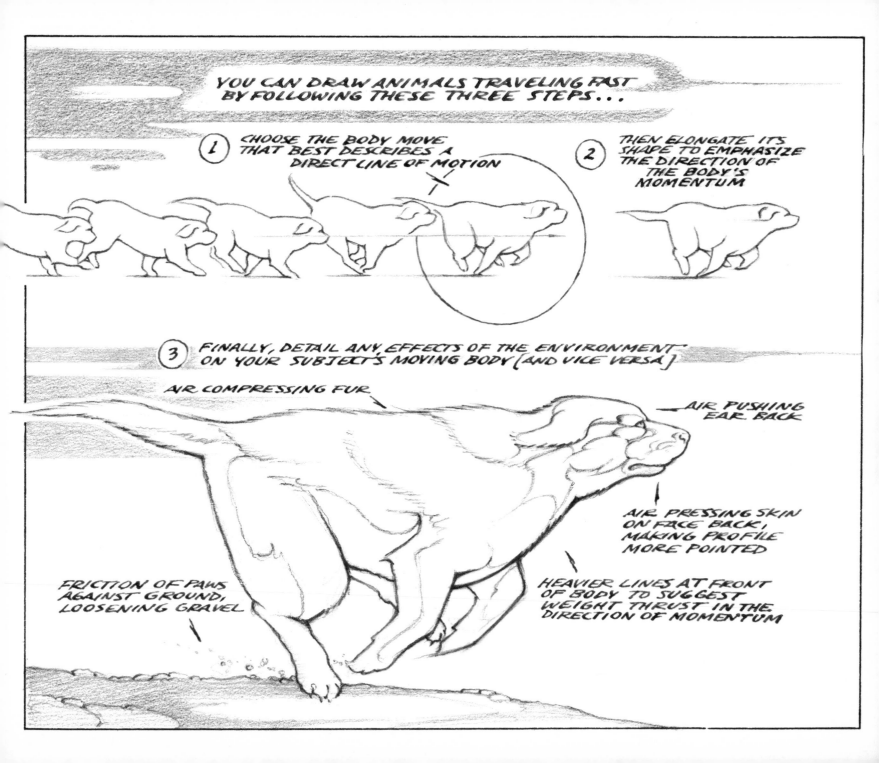

Look at the variety of living things and the diversity of their movements.

Everything you see can be drawn.

AN APPENDIX OF PHOTOGRAPHS
BY TED LEVIN

WITH CAPTIONS BY JIM ARNOSKY

Sketching in a meadow, I am surrounded by plants in perpetual motion. It is important to get close enough to notice details, such as how the tendrils of the vetch plant grasp the tall stems of these Black-eyed Susans.

I like to go sketching directly after a rain. Plants full of moisture appear more vivid. Buds open. Stems stretch. Leaves twist to face the shifting light. Here a Wild Cucumber vine, laden with raindrops, reaches out to climb on whatever it can touch.

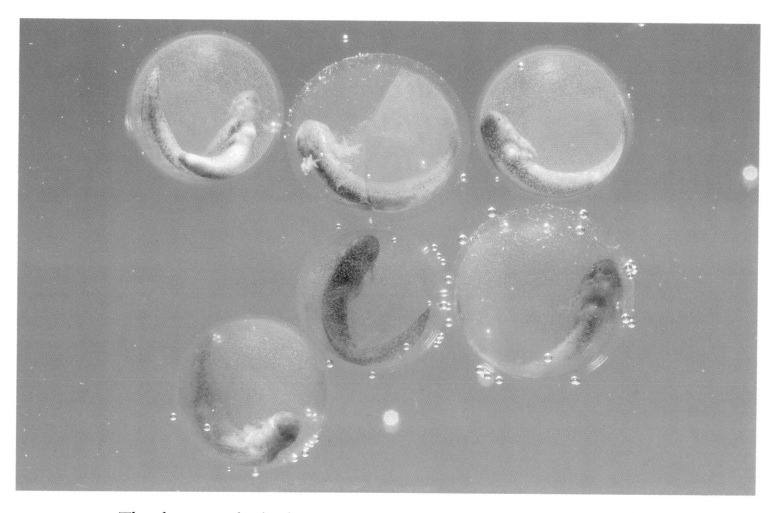

The closer you look, the more movement you are apt to see. A good magnifying glass will allow you to see small life close-up almost as well as you can see in these photographic enlargements. On the left, a mosquito struggles to escape the sticky hold of the insect-eating sundew plant. Above, salamander embryos are wriggling to hatch from their jellylike eggs.

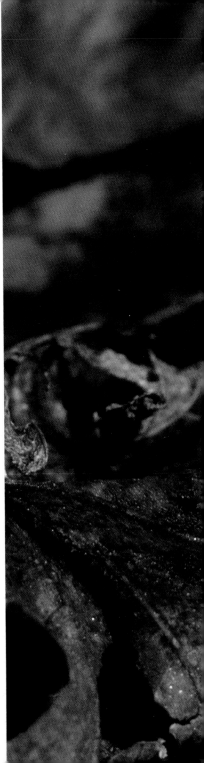

A lot can be learned about the ways animals move by studying the tracks they make. Tracks can tell you whether the animal was hopping, crawling, sliding, shuffling, waddling, stepping briskly, loping, or running.

Animals move by pushing and pulling themselves along. See how this Red Eft is using its limbs to pull and push itself through leaf litter.

A snake is a living line of motion.

Of all animals, mammals have the most expressive faces. Compare the face of this raccoon eating an acorn with that of the snake. When you watch mammals, notice how they use their face muscles when they call, growl, smell, taste, drink, or eat.

Look for minor changes in a bird's body—a tilt of the head, the spreading of some feathers, a slight shift of weight or lifting of a foot—and you will be able to perceive and draw even the slowest motions.

The quick, fluid motion of an otter as it emerges from a hole in the ice is clearly suggested by the curve of its outstretched neck and body.

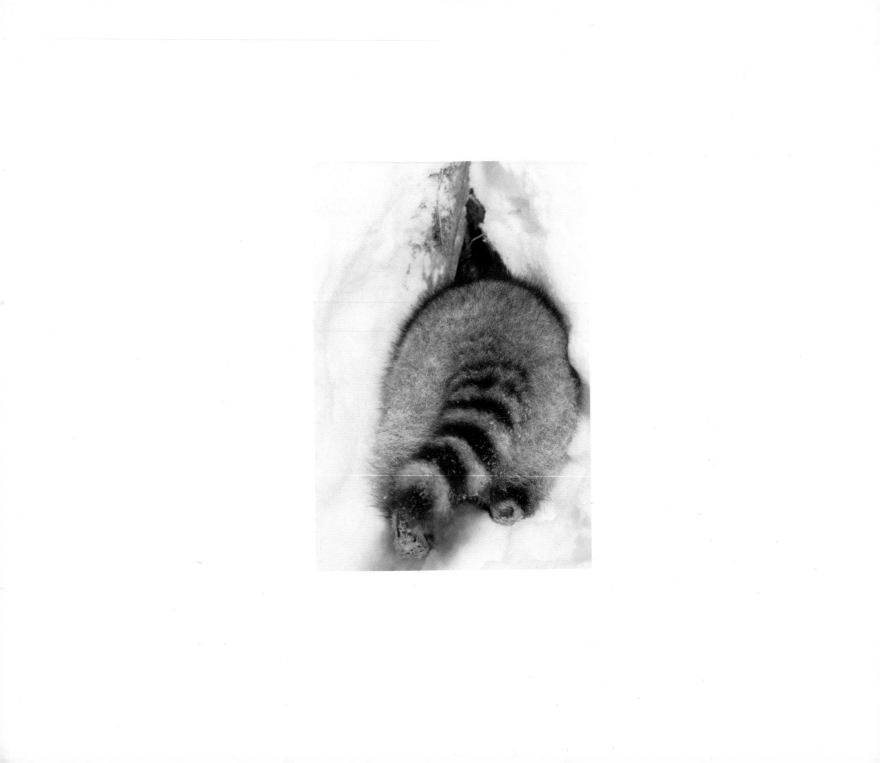